MW00880611

EASY TACO
COOKBOOK

THE EFFORTLESS CHEF SERIES

By
Chef Maggie Chow
Copyright © 2015 by Saxonberg
Associates

Published by
BookSumo, a division of Saxonberg
Associates
http://www.booksumo.com/

A GIFT FROM ME TO YOU...

Send the Book!

I know you like easy cooking. But what about Japanese Sushi?

Join my private reader's club and get a copy of **_Infinite Sushi: A Complete Set of Sushi and Japanese Recipes_** by fellow BookSumo author Hashimoto Kazuma for FREE!

<u>Send the Book!</u>

Enjoy some of the best sushi available!

You will also receive updates about all my new books when they are free. So please show your support.

Also don't forget to like and subscribe on the social networks. I love meeting my readers. Links to all my profiles are below so please click and connect :)

<u>Facebook</u>

<u>Twitter</u>

ABOUT THE AUTHOR.

Maggie Chow is the author and creator of your favorite *Easy Cookbooks* and *The Effortless Chef Series*. Maggie is a lover of all things related to food. Maggie loves nothing more than finding new recipes, trying them out, and then making them her own, by adding or removing ingredients, tweaking cooking times, and anything to make the recipe not only taste better, but be easier to cook!

For a complete listing of all my books please see my author page.

INTRODUCTION

Welcome to *The Effortless Chef Series*!
Thank you for taking the time to
download the *Easy Taco Cookbook*.
Come take a journey with me into the
delights of easy cooking. The point of
this cookbook and all my cookbooks is to
exemplify the effortless nature of
cooking simply.

In this book we focus on Tacos. You will
find that even though the recipes are
simple, the taste of the dishes is quite
amazing.

So will you join me in an adventure of
simple cooking? If the answer is yes
(and I hope it is) please consult the table
of contents to find the dishes you are
most interested in. Once you are ready
jump right in and start cooking.

— Chef Maggie Chow

TABLE OF CONTENTS

ANY ISSUES? CONTACT ME

If you find that something important to you is missing from this book please contact me at maggie@booksumo.com.

I will try my best to re-publish a revised copy taking your feedback into consideration and let you know when the book has been revised with you in mind.

:)

— Chef Maggie Chow

LEGAL NOTES

COMMON ABBREVIATIONS

cup(s)	C.
tablespoon	tbsp
teaspoon	tsp
ounce	oz
pound	lb

*All units used are standard American measurements

CHAPTER 1: EASY TACO RECIPES

EASY RICE FOR TACOS

Maggie's Thoughts: Enhance any taco recipe with this rice.

Ingredients

- 1 (14.5 oz.) can chicken broth
- 1 (8 oz.) can tomato sauce
- 1 (1 oz.) package taco seasoning mix
- 1 1/2 C. uncooked instant rice
- 1 (6 oz.) can black olives, drained and chopped
- 1 C. shredded Cheddar cheese
- 1 C. sour cream

Directions

- Boil the following in a saucepan: taco seasoning, chicken broth, and tomato sauce.
- Once the broth is boiling add your rice to the pot. Place a lid on it and shut off the heat. Let the rice sit for 7 mins.
- Finally add in your olives and cheese. Combine everything evenly. Then top with some sour cream before serving.
- Enjoy.

Amount per serving (4 total)

Timing Information:

Preparation	Cooking	Total Time
5 m	10 m	15 m

Nutritional Information:

Calories	459 kcal
Fat	26.4 g
Carbohydrates	42.6g
Protein	12.7 g
Cholesterol	55 mg
Sodium	1392 mg

* Percent Daily Values are based on a 2,000 calorie diet.

TACO I

(JALAPENO BEER BATTERED FISH)

Ingredients

- 1 C. all-purpose flour
- 2 tbsps cornstarch
- 1 tsp baking powder
- 1/2 tsp salt
- 1 egg
- 1 C. beer
- 1/2 C. plain yogurt
- 1/2 C. mayonnaise
- 1 lime, juiced
- 1 jalapeno pepper, minced
- 1 tsp minced capers
- 1/2 tsp dried oregano
- 1/2 tsp ground cumin
- 1/2 tsp dried dill weed
- 1 tsp ground cayenne pepper
- 1 quart oil for frying

- 1 lb cod fillets, cut into 2 to 3 oz. portions
- 1 (12 oz.) package corn tortillas
- 1/2 medium head cabbage, finely shredded

Directions

- Add oil to a big frying pot or deep fryer and get it to 375 degrees.
- Blend the following in your blender until smooth: beer and eggs. Put everything into a bowl.
- Get a 2nd bowl, evenly mix: salt, flour, baking powder, and cornstarch.
- Combine both bowls and stir to get an even batter.
- Get a 3rd bowl, mix: mayo, lime juice, cayenne, jalapenos, dill, capers, cumin, yogurt, and oregano.
- Coat your fish with some flour and enter it into the batter. Fry until crispy then remove excess

oil with some paper towels. Then
fry the tortillas.

- Layer some fish, then some
  cabbage, and finally some mayo
  sauce on each tortilla.
- Enjoy.

Amount per serving (8 total)

Timing Information:

Preparation	Cooking	Total Time
40 m	20 m	1 h

Nutritional Information:

Calories	409 kcal
Fat	18.8 g
Carbohydrates	43g
Protein	17.3 g
Cholesterol	54 mg
Sodium	407 mg

* Percent Daily Values are based on a 2,000 calorie diet.

Taco II

(Jalapeno Lime Sirloin)

Ingredients

- 2 lbs top sirloin steak, cut into thin strips
- salt and ground black pepper to taste
- 1/4 C. vegetable oil
- 18 (6 inch) corn tortillas
- 1 onion, diced
- 4 fresh jalapeno peppers, seeded and chopped
- 1 bunch fresh cilantro, chopped
- 4 limes, cut into wedges

Directions

- Stir fry your steak for 6 mins. Then coat it with some pepper and salt. Set it aside.

- Add more oil to the pan and fry your tortillas.
- Layer cilantro, steak, jalapenos, and onions on each fried tortilla and then garnish with some lime.
- Enjoy.

Amount per serving (9 total)

Timing Information:

Preparation	Cooking	Total Time
15 m	10 m	25 m

Nutritional Information:

Calories	379 kcal
Fat	21.4 g
Carbohydrates	28.1g
Protein	20.3 g
Cholesterol	58 mg
Sodium	69 mg

* Percent Daily Values are based on a 2,000 calorie diet.

TACO III

(SWISS CHARD AND ONIONS)

Ingredients

- 1 1/2 tbsps olive oil
- 1 large onion, cut into 1/4-inch slices
- 3 cloves garlic, minced
- 1 tbsp red pepper flakes, or to taste
- 1/2 C. chicken broth
- 1 bunch Swiss chard, tough stems removed and leaves cut crosswise into 1 1/2-inch slices
- 1 pinch salt
- 12 corn tortillas
- 1 C. crumbled queso fresco cheese
- 3/4 C. salsa

Directions

- Stir fry your onions for 11 mins and then combine in some red pepper flakes, and garlic and cook for another 2 mins.
- Add into the onions: salt, chicken broth, and Swiss chard.
- Place a lid on the pan and set the heat to low. Simmer for 7 mins.
- Take off the lid and raise the heat a bit. Stir the contents for 6 mins until no liquid remains.
- Shut off the heat fully.
- Get a 2nd pan and toast the tortillas for 2 mins each side with a low level of heat.
- Layer queso fresco cheese, chard mix, and salsa on each tortilla.
- Enjoy.

Amount per serving (4 total)

Timing Information:

Preparation	Cooking	Total Time
20 m	45 m	1 h 5 m

Nutritional Information:

Calories	354 kcal
Fat	13 g
Carbohydrates	48.8g
Protein	14.4 g
Cholesterol	20 mg
Sodium	531 mg

* Percent Daily Values are based on a 2,000 calorie diet.

TACO IV

(GUACAMOLE AND TOMATOES)

Ingredients

- 1 (14.5 oz.) can whole tomatoes, drained, rinsed, patted dry
- 2 roma tomatoes, quartered
- 1 onion, chopped, divided
- 1 clove garlic, coarsely chopped
- 1/4 C. fresh cilantro
- 1/2 jalapeno pepper
- salt and pepper to taste
- 4 avocados, halved with pits removed
- 12 (6 inch) whole wheat tortillas
- 1 (15 oz.) can kidney beans, rinsed and drained
- 2 C. torn romaine lettuce

Directions

- Set your oven to 350 degrees before doing anything else.
- Enter the following into a blender or processor: jalapenos, fresh and canned tomatoes, garlic, and half of your onions.
- Process or pulse a few times. Do not make a smooth mix. Only dice the contents a bit.
- Get a bowl, mix until smooth: pepper, the rest of the onions, salt, and avocados.
- Get a casserole dish and cook your tortillas in the oven for 5 mins.
- Layer on each tortilla: lettuce, guacamole, salsa, and beans.
- Enjoy.

Amount per serving (6 total)

Timing Information:

Preparation	Cooking	Total Time
15 m	5 m	20 m

Nutritional Information:

Calories	455 kcal
Fat	21.1 g
Carbohydrates	70.1g
Protein	13.8 g
Cholesterol	0 mg
Sodium	604 mg

* Percent Daily Values are based on a 2,000 calorie diet.

Taco V

(Coleslaw)

Ingredients

- 1/2 small head cabbage, chopped
- 1 jalapeno pepper, seeded and minced
- 1/2 red onion, minced
- 1 carrot, chopped
- 1 tbsp chopped fresh cilantro
- 1 lime, juiced

Directions

- Simply combine all the ingredients in a bowl.
- Enjoy on warm tortillas with your choice of meat and salsa.

Amount per serving (6 total)

Timing Information:

Preparation	Cooking	Total Time
20 m		20 m

Nutritional Information:

Calories	27 kcal
Fat	0.1 g
Carbohydrates	6.6g
Protein	1.1 g
Cholesterol	0 mg
Sodium	19 mg

* Percent Daily Values are based on a 2,000 calorie diet.

TACO VI

(CORN AND BEEF)

Ingredients

- 2 lbs ground beef
- 1 onion, chopped
- 2 (15 oz.) cans ranch-style beans
- 1 (15.25 oz.) can whole kernel corn
- 1 (10 oz.) can diced tomatoes with green chile peppers
- 1 (14.5 oz.) can peeled and diced tomatoes with juice
- 1 (1.25 oz.) package taco seasoning mix

Directions

- Cook your onions and beef for 10 mins then remove oil excesses.
- Combine with the beef your chili peppers, beans, taco seasoning,

tomatoes, and corn. Stir the contents for a min. Cook over medium heat for 17 mins.

- Enjoy.

Amount per serving (8 total)

Timing Information:

Preparation	Cooking	Total Time
15 m	30 m	45 m

Nutritional Information:

Calories	520 kcal
Fat	30.7 g
Carbohydrates	32.6g
Protein	26.7 g
Cholesterol	96 mg
Sodium	1289 mg

* Percent Daily Values are based on a 2,000 calorie diet.

Taco VII

(Shrimp and Cilantro)

Ingredients

- 1 mango - peeled, seeded and diced
- 1 ripe avocado - peeled, pitted, and diced
- 2 tomatoes, diced
- 1/2 C. chopped fresh cilantro
- 1/4 C. chopped red onion
- 3 cloves garlic, minced
- 1/2 tsp salt
- 2 tbsps lime juice
- 1/4 C. honey butter
- 1 lb salad shrimp
- 4 (10 inch) flour tortillas, warmed

Directions

- Get bowl combine: lime juice, mango, salt, avocadoes, garlic,

onions, and cilantro. Place a lid
or some plastic wrap on the bowl.

- Put the bowl in the fridge for 40
  mins.
- Stir fry your shrimp for 4 mins in
  the honey butter.
- Layer on your tortillas: mango
  mix, and shrimp.
- Enjoy.

Amount per serving (4 total)

Timing Information:

Preparation	Cooking	Total Time
15 m	2 m	47 m

Nutritional Information:

Calories	567 kcal
Fat	23.1 g
Carbohydrates	59.5g
Protein	31.2 g
Cholesterol	188 mg
Sodium	951 mg

* Percent Daily Values are based on a 2,000 calorie diet.

TACO VIII

(TERIYAKI STEAK)

Ingredients

- 4 Mission(R) Soft Taco Flour Tortillas
- 8 oz. sirloin steak, chopped into 1x1/4-inch pieces
- 1/2 C. teriyaki marinade
- 1/2 C. cucumber, grated
- 1/2 C. carrots, shredded
- 1/2 tsp fresh ginger, grated
- 1/2 tsp black sesame seeds
- 1 tbsp fresh orange juice
- 1/2 tsp soy sauce
- 1/2 tsp honey
- Salt and pepper to taste
- 1/2 C. sliced green onions

Directions

- Get a bowl, mix: teriyaki and steak.
- Place a lid on the container and put it in the fridge for 30 mins.
- Get a 2nd bowl, combine: honey, pepper, cucumbers, ginger, soy sauce, carrots, sesame seeds, salt, and orange juice.
- Put this in the fridge as well with a covering until you are ready to assemble your tacos.
- Stir fry your steak and marinade for 12 mins.
- Layer the following on each tortillas: sliced green onions, one fourth C. of carrot mix, and an even amount of steak.

Amount per serving (2 total)

Timing Information:

Preparation	Cooking	Total Time
30 m	10 m	40 m

Nutritional Information:

Calories	465 kcal
Fat	15 g
Carbohydrates	69.7g
Protein	33.2 g
Cholesterol	49 mg
Sodium	3853 mg

* Percent Daily Values are based on a 2,000 calorie diet.

Taco IX

(Cheddar Beef)

Ingredients

- 10 fluid oz. warm water
- 3/4 tsp salt
- 3 tbsps vegetable oil
- 4 C. all-purpose flour
- 2 tsps active dry yeast
- 1 (6 oz.) can tomato paste
- 3/4 C. water
- 1 (1.25 oz.) package taco seasoning mix, divided
- 1 tsp chili powder, or to taste
- 1/2 tsp cayenne pepper, or to taste
- 1 (16 oz.) can fat-free refried beans
- 1/3 C. salsa
- 1/4 C. chopped onion
- 1/2 lb ground beef
- 4 C. shredded Cheddar cheese

Directions

- Enter the following into a bread machine: yeast, water, flour, oil, and salt.
- Use the dough cycle.
- Occasionally check the dough to make sure it is not too dry if so add some water.
- Get a bowl, mix: 3/4 taco seasoning, cayenne pepper, water chili powder, and tomato paste.
- Get a 2nd bowl, mix: onions, salsa, and refried beans.
- Set your oven to 400 degrees before doing anything else.
- Stir fry your ground beef remove oil excesses. Then put some water and the rest of the taco seasoning.
- Let the contents simmer for 4 mins then shut the heat.
- Take your dough, once the machine is done, and break it into two pieces.

- Flatten the dough into two 12 inch circular layers.
- On each dough piece layer: tomato mix, bean mix, beef, and cheese.
- Cook in the oven for 17 mins.
- After 7 mins turn the contents.

Amount per serving (16 total)

Timing Information:

Preparation	Cooking	Total Time
2 h	20 m	2 h 20 m

Nutritional Information:

Calories	338 kcal
Fat	16.1 g
Carbohydrates	32.7g
Protein	14.8 g
Cholesterol	42 mg
Sodium	708 mg

* Percent Daily Values are based on a 2,000 calorie diet.

TACO X

(BEANS AND WHITE RICE I)

Ingredients

- 3 tomatoes, seeded and chopped
- 2 avocados, chopped
- 1 small onion, chopped
- 1/4 C. chopped fresh cilantro
- 2 cloves garlic, minced
- 1 lime, juiced
- 2 tbsps vegetable oil
- 8 corn tortillas
- 1 (15 oz.) can black beans, drained and rinsed
- 1 C. cooked white rice
- 2 tbsps chopped fresh cilantro
- 1 dash green pepper sauce

Directions

- Get a bowl, combine then toss: garlic, tomatoes, lime juice, one fourth C. cilantro, onions, and avocados.

- For 2 mins per side cook your tortillas in veggie oil.
- Layer on each tortilla: 2 tbsps of beans, tomato mix, 2 tbsps of cilantro and green pepper sauce, 2 tbsps of cooked rice.
- Enjoy.

Amount per serving (4 total)

Timing Information:

Preparation	Cooking	Total Time
15 m	10 m	25 m

Nutritional Information:

Calories	512 kcal
Fat	23.7 g
Carbohydrates	67.2g
Protein	13.7 g
Cholesterol	0 mg
Sodium	448 mg

* Percent Daily Values are based on a 2,000 calorie diet.

TACO XI

(TEMPEH AND VEGGIE BROTH)

Ingredients

- 2 tbsps extra virgin olive oil
- 1 small onion, minced
- 2 cloves garlic, minced
- 1 (8 oz.) package spicy flavored tempeh, coarsely grated
- 1/2 C. vegetable broth
- 2 tbsps taco seasoning mix
- 1 tsp dried oregano
- 1/2 tsp ground red pepper (optional)

Directions

- Stir fry your onions for 6 mins in oil. Combine in garlic and cook for another 3 mins. Add in your tempeh and cook for 6 more mins.

- Add in the veggie broth to the onions, add in the taco seasoning, red pepper, and oregano.
- Lower the heat and let the mix cook until all the liquid is removed. This should take about 7 mins.
- Layer the mix on tacos or tortillas.
- Enjoy.

Amount per serving (4 total)

Timing Information:

Preparation	Cooking	Total Time
15 m	15 m	30 m

Nutritional Information:

Calories	199 kcal
Fat	13 g
Carbohydrates	11.4g
Protein	10.9 g
Cholesterol	0 mg
Sodium	392 mg

* Percent Daily Values are based on a 2,000 calorie diet.

TACO XII

(SOFT AND HARD SHELL)

Ingredients

- 1 1/4 lbs ground beef
- 1/2 onion, chopped
- 1 (1.25 oz.) package dry taco seasoning mix
- 3/4 C. water
- 1 (14 oz.) can refried beans
- 4 oz. process cheese food (such as Velveeta(R)), cut into small cubes
- 10 (6 inch) flour tortillas, warmed
- 10 crisp taco shells, warmed

Directions

- For 11 mins fry your onions and beef. Then remove any excess oils.
- Get a saucepan and add water and taco seasoning.

- Get this mixture boiling.
- Once boiling lower the heat and let it simmer for 12 mins.
- After 12 mins combine the taco seasoning mix with the beef and let the contents continue to lightly boil.
- Get a 2nd saucepan and mix cubed cheese and refried beans together. Heat for 10 mins stir and heat for 12 more mins.
- Layer each tortilla with an equal amount of refried beans and cheese. Fold each tortilla around a taco.
- Then add in your seasoned ground beef.

Amount per serving (10 total)

Timing Information:

Preparation	Cooking	Total Time
10 m	20 m	30 m

Nutritional Information:

Calories	347 kcal
Fat	16 g
Carbohydrates	31.9g
Protein	17.5 g
Cholesterol	49 mg
Sodium	801 mg

* Percent Daily Values are based on a 2,000 calorie diet.

Taco XIII

(Corn Beef and Coleslaw)

Ingredients

- 2 C. plain yogurt
- 1/2 C. mayonnaise
- 1 lime, juiced
- 2 tbsps chopped fresh cilantro
- 1 pinch cayenne pepper, or to taste
- salt to taste
- 1 1/2 C. shredded corned beef
- 8 (10 inch) flour tortillas
- 1 lb prepared coleslaw

Directions

- Get combine the following evenly: salt, yogurt, cayenne, cilantro, and lime juice.
- Warm your corned beef in a pan.

- Warm your tortillas in another pan for 1 min per side.
- Layer on each tortilla 3 tbsps of beef with 2 tbsps of slaw.
- Garnish with 2 tbsps of mayo mix.
- Enjoy.

Amount per serving (8 total)

Timing Information:

Preparation	Cooking	Total Time
15 m	10 m	25 m

Nutritional Information:

Calories	433 kcal
Fat	20.2 g
Carbohydrates	48.9g
Protein	14.1 g
Cholesterol	27 mg
Sodium	867 mg

* Percent Daily Values are based on a 2,000 calorie diet.

Taco XIV

(Spicy Eggplant)

Ingredients

- 1/4 C. olive oil, divided
- 1 small onion, chopped
- 2 tbsps lemon juice
- 2 cloves fresh garlic, minced
- 1/4 jalapeno pepper, minced
- 1 eggplant, cut into cubes
- 2 tbsps ground cumin
- 1 tbsp paprika
- 1 1/2 tsps chili powder
- 1 tsp ground black pepper
- 1/2 tsp seasoned salt (such as Johnny's Seasoning Salt(R))
- 4 taco shells

Directions

- Stir fry the following in 2 tbsps of olive oil for 5 mins: jalapenos, onions, garlic, and lemon juice.
- Then add the following to the mix: salt, eggplants, pepper, cumin, remaining olive oil, chili powder, and paprika.
- Cook for 16 mins on a low to medium heat.
- Layer the mix on warm tortillas.
- Enjoy.

Amount per serving (4 total)

Timing Information:

Preparation	Cooking	Total Time
15 m	20 m	35 m

Nutritional Information:

Calories	255 kcal
Fat	18 g
Carbohydrates	23.3g
Protein	3.8 g
Cholesterol	0 mg
Sodium	193 mg

* Percent Daily Values are based on a 2,000 calorie diet.

Taco XV

(Black Bean and Bacon)

Ingredients

- 1 C. water
- 1/2 C. white rice
- 5 slices bacon
- 1 (14 oz.) can black beans
- 2 tsps taco seasoning mix, divided
- 1 tsp vegetable oil, or as needed
- 5 flour tortillas
- 2 tomatoes, diced
- 1 green bell pepper, chopped
- 1 C. shredded Cheddar cheese

Directions

- Get a saucepan add in water, get it boiling, and then add in rice.
- Place a lid on the pan, set the heat to low, and let the rice cook for 22 mins.

- Set your oven to 250 degrees before doing anything else.
- Fry your bacon for 11 mins.
- Then it place to the side on paper towels to remove excess fat and then break the bacon into pieces.
- Keep the oils from the bacon in the pan.
- Get a saucepan and mix together 1 tsp of taco seasoning and your beans together. Cook for five mins.
- Add your rice to the pan with the bacon fat and also add in 1 teaspoon of taco seasoning.
- Stir everything well while heating the contents for about 4 mins.
- Get a baking dish and layer your tortillas in it. Coat the tortillas with some veggie oil. Cook them in the oven for 6 mins.
- Layer the following on each tortilla: rice mix, bean mix, cheddar cheese, bacon, green bell peppers, and tomatoes.
- Enjoy.

Amount per serving (5 total)

Timing Information:

Preparation	Cooking	Total Time
20 m	30 m	50 m

Nutritional Information:

Calories	573 kcal
Fat	24.9 g
Carbohydrates	60.2g
Protein	26.7 g
Cholesterol	61 mg
Sodium	1148 mg

* Percent Daily Values are based on a 2,000 calorie diet.

Taco XVI

(Beef Lengua)

Ingredients

- 1 beef tongue
- 2 tomatoes, diced
- 1 onion, diced
- 1 bunch fresh cilantro, chopped
- 1 tbsp vegetable oil
- salt and pepper to taste
- 6 (6 inch) corn tortillas
- 3 tbsps lemon juice

Directions

- Boil your beef in water for 50 mins for each lb.
- Let the beef cool, and then remove the outside skin, and any fat.
- Dice up the tongue for later.

- Get a bowl, and mix: cilantro, tomatoes, and onions.
- Fry your beef tongue in oil for 10 mins after adding some pepper and salt to it until browned nicely.
- Get a 2nd pan and for 2 mins per side warm your tortillas.
- Layer on each tortilla an equal amount tomatoes and beef,
- Garnish with lemon juice.
- Enjoy.

Amount per serving (6 total)

Timing Information:

Preparation	Cooking	Total Time
20 m	11 m	3 h

Nutritional Information:

Calories	566 kcal
Fat	40.1 g
Carbohydrates	15.9g
Protein	34.2 g
Cholesterol	218 mg
Sodium	126 mg

* Percent Daily Values are based on a 2,000 calorie diet.

Taco XVII

(Angel Hair Pasta)

Ingredients

- 1 (16 oz.) package angel hair pasta
- 1 (28 oz.) jar spaghetti sauce
- 1 (5.8 oz.) package crisp taco shells
- 1/4 C. grated Parmesan cheese

Directions

- Cook your angel hair in boiling water and salt for 6 mins until al dente.
- Remove all liquid from the pot.
- Put the pasta back in the pot with sauce and heat everything back up.
- Warm your taco shells for 1 min in the microwave.

- Add pasta to the tacos and garnish with 1 tsp of parmesan.
- Enjoy.

Amount per serving (12 total)

Timing Information:

Preparation	Cooking	Total Time
5 m	15 m	20 m

Nutritional Information:

Calories	236 kcal
Fat	6.2 g
Carbohydrates	38.5g
Protein	6.8 g
Cholesterol	3 mg
Sodium	425 mg

* Percent Daily Values are based on a 2,000 calorie diet.

TACO XVIII

(PUMPKIN AND AVOCADO)

Ingredients

- 2 tbsps vegetable oil
- 2 C. cubed fresh pumpkin
- 1/2 C. vegetable stock
- 1 tbsp ground cumin
- salt and ground black pepper to taste
- 12 flour or corn tortillas, warmed
- 3/4 C. diced fresh tomato
- 1/2 C. diced onion
- 1/2 C. diced ripe avocado
- 3 tbsps chopped fresh cilantro

Directions

- Stir fry your pumpkin for 5 mins in hot oil. Then add in your pepper, salt, veggie stock and cumin.

- Cook for 10 mins.
- Layer the following on your tortillas: pumpkin mix, cilantro, tomato, avocado, and onions.
- Enjoy as a taco.

Amount per serving (12 total)

Timing Information:

Preparation	Cooking	Total Time
25 m	7 m	32 m

Nutritional Information:

Calories	100 kcal
Fat	4.1 g
Carbohydrates	14.9g
Protein	2.1 g
Cholesterol	0 mg
Sodium	34 mg

* Percent Daily Values are based on a 2,000 calorie diet.

Taco XIX

(Pork and Chili)

Ingredients

- 1 lb cubed or minced pork stew meat
- 1 (1.25 oz.) package taco seasoning mix
- 1 tbsp vegetable oil
- 1 C. chunky salsa
- 1 (16 oz.) can chili beans, undrained
- 1/3 C. apricot preserves
- 12 taco shells
- 1 (10 oz.) can sliced ripe olives, for topping

Directions

- Get a resealable bag and mix: taco seasoning and pork. Shake the bag so everything gets coated nicely.

- Fry the pork until completely cooked in the oil.
- Add in apricots, beans, and salsa.
- Set the heat to low and let the contents lightly simmer for 12 mins.
- Add an even amount of mix to each taco and garnish with olives before serving.
- Enjoy.

Amount per serving (12 total)

Timing Information:

Preparation	Cooking	Total Time
5 m	25 m	30 m

Nutritional Information:

Calories	286 kcal
Fat	13.9 g
Carbohydrates	30.4g
Protein	11.3 g
Cholesterol	23 mg
Sodium	817 mg

* Percent Daily Values are based on a 2,000 calorie diet.

Taco XX

(Pork and Potatoes)

Ingredients

- 1 lb ground pork
- 3 red potatoes
- salt and pepper to taste
- 8 taco shells
- 1 C. iceberg lettuce, shredded
- 1 C. chopped fresh tomato
- 1/4 C. sour cream

Directions

- Fry your pork in oil until cooked but not fully done.
- Dice up your potatoes and mix them with the pork.
- Add enough water to the pot to coat the bottom of the pan and place lid on the pan and let the

potatoes and pork cook for 18 to 22 mins.

- Add in your preferred amount of pepper and salt.
- Put an equal amount of pork and potatoes into your taco shells and top with tomatoes, sour crema and lettuce.
- Enjoy.

Amount per serving (8 total)

Timing Information:

Preparation	Cooking	Total Time
10 m	30 m	50 m

Nutritional Information:

Calories	324 kcal
Fat	18.1 g
Carbohydrates	27.3g
Protein	13.1 g
Cholesterol	44 mg
Sodium	124 mg

* Percent Daily Values are based on a 2,000 calorie diet.

Taco XXI

(Easy Ground Beef)

Ingredients

- 1 lb ground beef
- 1 (12 oz.) bag mix vegetables
- 1 (11.04 oz.) box taco dinner kit
- 1/4 C. water
- Sour cream
- Shredded lettuce

Directions

- Cook your beef in a pan then remove any excess oils.
- Add in your taco seasoning, vegetables, and the water.
- Place a lid on the pan and cook for 7 mins or until you find that the veggies are soft.

- Add an equal amount to each taco or tortilla with some sour cream, taco sauce, and lettuce.
- Enjoy.

Amount per serving (4 total)

Timing Information:

Preparation	Cooking	Total Time
10 m	15 m	25 m

Nutritional Information:

Calories	519 kcal
Fat	25.1 g
Carbohydrates	43.5g
Protein	26.5 g
Cholesterol	77 mg
Sodium	1272 mg

* Percent Daily Values are based on a 2,000 calorie diet.

TACO XXII

(ITALIAN SAUSAGE AND BEEF)

Ingredients

- 1/2 lb Italian sausage
- 1 lb ground beef
- 1 (16 oz.) jar tomato pasta sauce
- 1 tsp sugar
- 16 taco shells, heated
- 3 C. shredded mozzarella cheese
- 1 tbsp dried Italian seasoning

Directions

- Fry your sausage and beef in a pan and then remove any excess oils.
- Add in your Italian seasonings.
- Get a saucepan and add your pasta sauce to it.

- When the sauce is simmering add your sugar and stir until all the sugar is dissolved.
- Add some beef and sausage to each taco and then top with some tomato sauce, and finally add a layer of mozzarella.
- Enjoy.

Amount per serving (16 total)

Timing Information:

Preparation	Cooking	Total Time
5 m	20 m	25 m

Nutritional Information:

Calories	262 kcal
Fat	14.5 g
Carbohydrates	18.5g
Protein	13.8 g
Cholesterol	37 mg
Sodium	462 mg

* Percent Daily Values are based on a 2,000 calorie diet.

TACO XXIII

(CHEDDAR SOUP)

Ingredients

- 1 lb ground beef
- 1 medium onion, chopped
- 1/2 tsp chili powder
- 1 (10.75 oz.) can Campbell's(R) Condensed Fiesta Nacho Cheese Soup
- 8 taco shells, warmed
- 1 C. shredded lettuce
- 1 medium tomato, chopped

Directions

- Fry your onions, beef, and chili powder until the beef is fully done.
- Remove any oil excesses from the pan.

- Add half a C. of soup and get the soup simmering. Then shut off the heat.
- Warm the rest of the soup in a separate pan until also simmering. Shut off the heat again.
- Put your preferred amount of beef mix into each taco and then top with some more warmed soup mix.
- Enjoy.

Amount per serving (8 total)

Timing Information:

Preparation	Cooking	Total Time
10 m	15 m	25 m

Nutritional Information:

Calories	219 kcal
Fat	12.5 g
Carbohydrates	14.7g
Protein	11.9 g
Cholesterol	39 mg
Sodium	337 mg

* Percent Daily Values are based on a 2,000 calorie diet.

TACO XXIV

(VEGETARIAN)

Ingredients

- 3 avocados - peeled, pitted, and mashed
- 1/4 C. onions, diced
- 1/4 tsp garlic salt
- 12 (6 inch) corn tortillas
- 1 bunch fresh cilantro leaves, finely chopped
- jalapeno pepper sauce, to taste

Directions

- Set your oven to 325 degrees before doing anything else.
- Get a bowl and evenly mix: garlic salt, onions, and avocados.
- Heat your taco shells in the oven in a baking dish for 6 mins.

- Then add an equal amount of avocados to each shell.
- Top with some jalapeno sauce, and cilantro.
- Enjoy.

Amount per serving (6 total)

Timing Information:

Preparation	Cooking	Total Time
20 m	5 m	25 m

Nutritional Information:

Calories	279 kcal
Fat	16.3 g
Carbohydrates	32.8g
Protein	5.3 g
Cholesterol	0 mg
Sodium	111 mg

* Percent Daily Values are based on a 2,000 calorie diet.

A GIFT FROM ME TO YOU...

Send the Book!

I know you like easy cooking. But what about Japanese Sushi?

Join my private reader's club and get a copy of ***Infinite Sushi: A Complete Set of Sushi and Japanese Recipes*** by fellow BookSumo author Hashimoto Kazuma for FREE!

Send the Book!

Enjoy some of the best sushi available!

You will also receive updates about all my new books when they are free. So please show your support.

Also don't forget to like and subscribe on the social networks. I love meeting my readers. Links to all my profiles are below so please click and connect :)

Facebook

Twitter

COME ON...
LET'S BE FRIENDS :)

I adore my readers and love connecting with them socially. Please follow the links below so we can connect on Facebook, Twitter, and Google+.

Facebook

Twitter

I also have a blog that I regularly update for my readers so check it out below.

My Blog

Can I Ask A Favour?

If you found this book interesting, or have otherwise found any benefit in it. Then may I ask that you post a review of it on Amazon? Nothing excites me more than new reviews, especially reviews which suggest new topics for writing. I do read all reviews and I always factor feedback into my newer works.

So if you are willing to take ten minutes to write what you sincerely thought about this book then please visit our Amazon page and post your opinions.

Again thank you!

Interested in Other Easy Cookbooks?

Everything is easy! Check out my Amazon Author page for more great cookbooks:

For a complete listing of all my books please see my author page.

Made in the USA
Middletown, DE
16 June 2017